Après L'Amour

One Hundred One Poems

Après L'Amour
One Hundred One Poems
Copyright © 2017 Charles Triano

Cover art / photograph © C Triano

The Library of Congress © 2017

ISBN-10: 0-9987396-1-8
ISBN-13: 978-0-9987396-1-8

Charlie Triano
PO Box 543
Sausalito, CA
94966

beyond-destination@charlietriano.com
www.charlietriano.com

For Sharon

Also by Charlie Triano

Available on www.lulu.com

Beyond Destination ©
A Collection of Short Stories - Book One

A man with few regrets has less to write about.

C Triano

Après L'Amour

One Hundred One Poems

Charlie Triano

To all the suns so conquerable
To all our strengths so crucial
To every breath something magical
Though to each eventually the day falls

Le Jour Tombe
C Triano

Après L'Amour

On Enduring an Artistic Endeavor

I went through life unrecognized
Though content in my disguise

In the Dark

I sit in the dark
As I have many times
Many nights
Watching you sleep
Waiting for you
To move gently
Elegantly
Under the sheets
As I listen to you, breathe

I sit in the dark alone
Now that you've gone
Still waiting to hear
That familiar sound in my ear
Waiting for your breath
To fill the air
The rustle of your skin
Warm and bare, against me there
But it's only the darkness now
Crying out
As I lie here
Without you, now

Passages

With morning comes, it seems
A sound, a timbre, that tests the dream
Something intangible, though unmistakably foreseen
Sans kindness, almost obscene
Something in need of aspirin and Visine

With sleep still buried in my eyes
Like pus dried in a tempered wound
I awake, though more a view from a tomb
To a stale and suffocating room
One still draped in dubious choices
To seemingly distant and high pitched voices
Like the ones that rattled the old neighborhood
Not unlike a foreign enemy would
Embattled and misunderstood
Where women shout in shrilled accents
Over clotheslines with their backs bent
Stretched as if between two continents
Across the backs of buildings and wooden fence
Where children cry in discontent
And everything is as it's meant

But it's not the voices it seems
Through the ease of a summer's breeze
In July and august city streets
But something else indeed
So, rambling idle in my bed
Ready to dream, readying my head
I search for the voice, or rather the pitch
But its closer than that, closer than this
Closer than where most memories rest

It's like the cry of a lover's cue
Almost forgotten but for the bruise
Somewhere between sleep and bad judgment
Caught like breath in cuddled cadence
But I'm certain that was more coincidence

Like Catholics after catechism
Where boys box in gymnasiums
A kind of adolescent inquisition
Though more a slap, this is not that

So, I turn to find my empty skin
Is the only thing that's creeping in
Sagging like a sermon on sin
Spoken over, and over again
Without even a trace of Him

You lose a lover but not their fragrance
We can't deny where we bury our faces
Deep in soft necks and even cozier places
Not unlike the terry-cloth mother graces
As I snuggled in her linen and lace
As she read from a sizable page
Of fairy tales and other fates

But now it seems perhaps a scream
Coming from the next apartment
Cries from a virtual orgy of sexual assortment
Pounded walls, cracked and peeling
Mannequins reflected on bedroom ceilings
Images caught in mirrored glass
Images of passions past
A place where nothing's denied
And nothing lasts
Here, hold my breath, I'll be right back

But then with a burst, the iambic shrill reappears
Like something coming up from the rear
As it passes through dark and narrow passages
Not unlike a stack of unread messages

Though it's similar to a boyish thin-lipped whistle
Or that of a threatening Khrushchev missile
Like the one we imagined would echo and sizzle
Through the streets of Upper Manhattan

Where we waited, and waited for something to happen
Ducked and covered like lost lovers
Holding on to one another
But only a Spaulding conquered that early Sixties' sky
A little pink ball thrown on the fly
Passing through a time when nearly everything died

It's the lips that make life so sweet
Listening for sounds we think we need
The words we speak, what we believe
And the kisses caught somewhere in between
A tender touch on my arm
Her hand still slightly warm
Her skirt a short love poem
That I couldn't quite read, I couldn't hold on

His fingers like a comb
As he whispered through my hair
Not much feels like home
But I'd die if I wasn't there

A kiss to the nape of the neck
Or to a place you wouldn't expect
Like being saved from a horrific car wreak
By the jaws of life from the jaws of death

Now I wonder if it's the phone in the other room
Am I late for something, or someone's rung too soon?
Or fire engines passing through the streets in ruin
The whining continues, I have laundry to do

In truth, it's more like wings cutting through
The humid air as I stood still
Abandoned at the airport gate, my ticket unused
Only to watch on the evening news
From my Miami motel room
How it all went down like a busted balloon
So much for shooting the moon
Or dreaming too soon

It takes these dozen thoughts to realize
That it's just my septum in disguise
Breathing through deviated passages
Like rats caught in prisons
I don't know why it is
That I still make these bad decisions
Something deep inside of me
Escaping me, denying me
A sound too close to recognize
A sound reflected in reddened eyes
The one I hear in all my lies,
It's everywhere, where days die

The Woman on The Window Settee

To the woman who sat
On the window settee
In 1970
Some miles, outside of Albany
Around the same time, Joni
Posed in a painter's gallery,
You looked just as lovely,
Sadly, you never offered me
Your beauty
The only thing I necked that night
Was your Guild guitar
Sweet and slender
As a woman's arm,
But I did all I could
To coax your charms,
Though in the end
All I'm left with
Is this love poem

Love

Nothing is more talked about
Or more written or acted out
And apparently,
It's something we can't live without

Though it can be treated rather casually
That is, until it becomes a casualty
Or the threat of its availability

Love is something we do to each other
Sometimes while waiting for another
Or while just wandering from lover to lover

Sometimes we just love for ourselves
Selfishly, and not someone else
Somehow, we think it helps

Love is where we go to, again and again
Expecting it to dampen the pain
But sometimes, it's far less a friend

Love is all kinds
It takes us, and makes us lose our mind
And it's often foolishly left behind

Love is strange to most of us
Some just can't seem to get enough
While others try, and call its bluff

Love can grow from a distance
Like a blooming flower on a fence
Balanced in a wind of hopeful intent

Though love can die, in that same distance
Wondering where's the romance
As it lingers, and dies of discontent

Ah Love, here it comes again
Like a champion in a boxing ring
Though more a sparring partner, than companion

Love is best viewed in hindsight
While sleeping alone on a quiet night
Realizing only then, why it didn't go right

Love can slowly slip from your grasp
While it snores, or sleeps in a facial mask
Some designs weren't meant to last

But love doesn't truly sleep
It tosses and turns, waiting to dream
Usually in a place where nothing's as it seems

Love can be found on its knees
Sometimes down there trying to please
Others praying there's more up its sleeve

Love always seems to test the seams
As it doesn't always know what it means
Though often misunderstood, and ready to bleed

Love,
Maybe we should just wait and walk awhile
Let me get to know your smile
And not the one you've cleverly applied
But the one that will eventually lie

Love,
Let's see if you can be denied
Or if you're just something
That's crossed my mind
And will disappear in time

Alpha Beta for Brautigan

A
Boy
Caught
Dreams
Eagerly
For
Girls
Held
Intrinsically
Joined
Kindheartedly
Like
Man's
Need
Of
Poetry
Quoted
Romantically
So
That
Uncanny
Visuals
Would
X-Ray
Your
Zs

As I Went By

So, few, just sit in the sun
Blindly reading someone
Else's writing, about the same
Without feigning focusing on a page
These days, in fashionable cafes

Most watch passersby
With a distracted, and curious eye
Wondering if life would be satisfied
If it ever found its full design

But there you sat, seriously content
There was no reason to turn your head
You just turned a well-read page instead

It was in your posture, your pose
In your abandoned peripherals
Letting things just come and go
Fully unaware of the flow

It was in your face, your hands, your very self
Portrayed alone, with no one else
A graceful wind through your hair
As you sat there, lost to the open air

Divested of vanity, you focused genuinely
Lost in thought, you hadn't even noticed me
Watching you doing nothing, deliberately
You were everything I wanted, and wanted to be

But I dared not spoil it, or intrude on it
(Was I even fit to dream it?)
Left to quietly worship it
I walked on, transformed by it

Dimensions of Death

(For Kay)

In my thoughts
I blindly
Get lost
I go through the motions
Glad that breathing's
An instinctive function

Sometimes I eat
It's just a distraction
An image before me
Strange colors
Stranger shapes
Survival without satisfaction

Death had one dimension
It was something abstract
Something on television
Fiction
With no real face
Certainly, no relatives

There's no laughter now
In this hereafter now
The tears from my soul
Fall
Into deaths dimensions
Where there is nothing at all

In the Pink

Here I stand, where I once would
Like walking thru the old neighborhood
Or wandering the halls of motherhood
In this playful arena of my childhood
A place where my manhood once stood
Where like wood, it firmly tried to get what it could
It's a strange place now, with stranger smells
Though certainly not disagreeable
Just foreign to this now narrowed nostril
Though here in my vacancy, alongside old memories
With accompanying and comforting mammary
It's all coming back to me
Perhaps I'll recline here for awhile
Against your seductively skewed smile
Articulating love, while wondering why
So much time has slipped by
But it's funny how we acclimate
To old and distant intimates
To old passions and interests
Like love balanced on the cusp of fate
Or longing for lips on that perfect date
But then, weren't they parting anyway?
Now I'm sure I'm far less lascivious
And no doubt far less curious
As I ponder a more pleasant purpose
In search of something less flirtatious
Though perhaps something just as momentous
But is it truly love,
Or just something we think of?
But now we've come to this again
My once close and dear old friend
Now I'm sure I'm far less talented
(As the bone now bends lower than then)
Though I'll make the best of it,
Hoping for a happy end

Someone Else

The more I look in the mirror
The stranger I seem to myself
The stranger I seem, the stranger I see
A stranger I see
I seem like someone else
The stranger I seem
It's someone else
The stranger I see
It seems like someone else
The stranger I see
Is someone else
Am I too hard on myself
Hell, I mean well
Perhaps I'm truly someone else
Can't tell, can you tell?
It seems like someone else
Is that me? That can't be me
Reflected in a broken dream
Is that me?
That can't be me
The face I see in the broken dream
Is that me?

I Wish I Could

…make that expression
You know the one, that…you know the one
You want to punch sometimes
Usually in dim lighting, and after a few drinks
Or that million-dollar grin
How could you not win with that one?
Or that look that feigned stupidity,
So delicately, so deliciously
That would come in handy

Some Things Remain

I thought of you today
Thought of you in romantic
And intrinsic ways
Perfumed in places I no longer stay
No less say or talk about
Places I'd forgotten about
Places I've done without
A time I've long since fallen from
A time between torn years
Dampened like a distant drum
A time last seen through tears
And depths of love that have disappeared

I thought of you, today
Knowing we'd never be again
But I doubt I'd still be the same champion
Not my word to explain
But one of your complimenting refrains
You were always endearing that way
Me, I wouldn't choose a hero's name
Especially with how things remain

Still, I thought of you today
You were still the same
Looking just as lovely in blue jeans
Still sitting somewhere in my dreams
Like the one I'd dreamt
While running in the rain
Or rather, while running away
Though luckily
Neither of us was caused much pain
I just wanted to say
I thought of you today
And that some things,
Still remain

This Road

I know this road, I know it well, the one I've traveled
The one I take to, time and time again
The one that takes me from tears to fame
The one that takes me to another just the same
This road I've traveled, I'll travel again
I know this road, and its attractions
Its fruit stands, and blooming passions
Its bumps and potholes, its crashes, and disasters
Even its green pastures, I've challenged in the rain
I know this road, and I'll travel it again, and again
I know this road; it's taken me for a loop or two
It's even taken me back to you
I know this road, and its signs
I've stood on it, and changed my mind
I've even stared at it, somewhat confused
As if wondering, what the weather would do
I know this road, and you know it too
I know, because I nearly, ran into you
Though this time, I swerved to pass the pain
But I know I'll see you on this road again
Before I come to that final bend
This road I know, I'll travel again, and again
I'll no doubt travel it,
Until the end

In Morning

The earth moves, the sun moves
The bowels move, the pen moves
The mind moves, through timeless dimensions
In the morning light, I sometimes
Want to push my face into your face
Or perhaps a more passionate place
A resting place, a place to taste
But sadly, I'm running late

Lips

It was his lips. It was always his lips.
It was only his lips I wanted to taste
For the first hour or so. They were so full,
And funny, and articulate. They were lovely and
Clever and, well, you get the idea of it.
They were powerful, and almost dissolvable
At least, with mine they were.
For just one kiss, I'd restrain myself, cause
It's always the lips, and how they kiss. But the wrong words,
Or a trace of vanity, and my passion abandons me
Perhaps not the same for someone else, but for me, well,
When they talk about themselves,
Endlessly, they lose me, no matter how I felt.
The lips expose the soul, it's the vehicle
By which it searches out the same
And come together again,
Truthfully, sincerely, miraculously
And when they pull on one another
And push apart, there's something
Still between them, still attached at the heart,
Perhaps even capturing constellations,
But the truth is always in the kiss,
Cause you can taste a lie,
It's bitter to the lips

Me or You

I'm not angry, just caught off-guard
Caught in the middle, emotionless now
But to tell you the truth
I'd nearly forgotten, all about it
Forgot how much I hated you
Or was it me, I wasn't into?
You see, I'd nearly forgotten all about it,
But that's what time will do

Miramar

We were talking about the pool the other day
The one in New York City
As I guess we do every year, as summer approaches
Siblings leaning on old memories, that seem much closer
We had season passes, those young summers
Where our parents dumped us, so as not to worry about us
But there was nowhere else we wanted to be, in that city
I remember our lockers
Large enough to walk into
Where we changed into our bathing suits
And big women too, vaccines like huge tattoos
I remember my youthful scars
And Terry the deaf lifeguard
His cool mirrored sunglasses
As he whistled at our raucous infractions
I remember being pushed into the deep end
And told to sink or swim
I remember racing across the hot sand
In search of shade, or perhaps a foreign land,
One surrounded by brownstone buildings
And several older siblings
Or under the empty picnic table
Where we'd wait until we were able,
To escape again, into another dream
I remember the athletic rings
And trying to swing like a gymnast in the wind
Or the parallel bars and the injuries
And the summer humidity
And of course, the smell of cars
I remember Pop's hotdog stand
Outside, when we left at six pm
Which we ate on the long way home
It seemed quicker getting there than getting back
(Aging is sort of like that)
We'll no doubt remember it again next year
And every year after that

I Forgot Things About You

I forget how you slept
This side, that side,
Toward me, away from me,
Into me
I forgot your breathing,
Your dreaming
I forgot your intentions, your touch
I forgot so much
Though I recall it was more than enough

I forgot that you slept
So peacefully
I forgot that you slept
So close to me
Holding me, like eternity
I forgot these things about you
Just as I forgot them about me

Say It First

That you love someone
And say it so you mean it
Say it first, before another says it
Exactly how you meant it
Don't let your words be stolen
Or worse, left in silence
With your thoughts, unheard
As they echo through the empty wind-
Believe me
The chance won't come again

My Mother's Hands

I can still see my mother's hands
The ones that helped me stand
The ones that helped me be a man
Which were strong and in demand,
The same ones that read to me,
And carried me to bed to dream
The only ones I'd ever need
The same ones that set me free
And that will always love me

The hands that emptied the dish rack
And perhaps even knew my father's back
As they scratched their way
To my conception
As he kissed her to perfection
But I doubt that would ever be,
Knowing my father and his breed
As his hands fought tempestuously
They were even known to make her bleed
We were children caught
Between domestic screams
Witnessing the death of parental dreams
Like a firing squad and last cigarette
Like the time,
Kennedy and Khrushchev met

And now as they lie lifelessly
My mother's hands still hold me
Undying in their generosity
Living forever
In my memory

Remembering You

I try to remember your body
Hoping not to confuse it with another
The body, not the lover
But it's far away now, that distant passion,
As it gradually fades from memory
Though I recall your thighs, as you walked by
My shirt barely covering your bottom,
An image that I've never forgotten
But sadly, we don't always see what we feel
In that dark embrace, in that poetic place
You see, I remember you mostly below the waist
Because, I'll never forget how you taste
Or our first date. Or even more, our first kiss
Because nothing we ever did
Would be more important than that,
More important than this

Closed Eyes

Closed eyes and confused,
I was seduced
By the very sight of you
By the simple thought of you
But if I searched for the truth
It was probably just the gin in the room
Either way, you were both rather cruel
You told me of your lovers
You told me of your sins in the sun
Lying, twisted under covers
You spoke in gentle whispers, like a gun
Now when we pass in the street
You're a million miles from me
Just another stranger at your feet
Nothing you'd ever need
Nothing you'd ever need

Anyone but You

I never really wanted to be,
Anyone but me
I never really wanted to believe,
That you couldn't love only me
There was no need for fantasy, I thought you knew
I never really wanted it to be, anyone but you
We turned the world into a room, torched by a Sinatra tune
Making love a sensuous perfume
Putting more than a man on the moon
(Love knows nothing of rules)
I watched you cry at Pere Lachaise
And tears of laughter in your sweet champagne
Or caught in a doorway on a rainy day
Your eyes were always sincerely the same
Here's my love, my testimony
I hope you find it's everything you need
It's more than words and a melody
I've bared all that's inside of me
Like carved initials in a tree
Our journey is caught in mystery
And if love's an endless dream
Then we 'll sleep for eternity

Nothing

Loneliness has crept in
Where love once had been
From nothing to everything
To nothing again
Where love once had been
There's nothing again
Where love once had been
There's nothing again
Nothing

Baby, It's You

The times have made a different man, of me,
Me
Figuring out the different love, I see
You see
I thought I'd get a line or two, from you,
For you
A hundred more still sing the blues,
I'd dream a life, a different night, without you,
You're more my mind than life is time
Baby, it's you

Baby it's you, who does all the loving
Baby it's you, who does all the suffering
Baby, it's you, who thinks nothing of it
Cause you know what it all means
And you say the funniest things
And somewhere between
A wild high and a wicked dream
Baby, you look lovely in blue jeans

One More Tear

There's one more tear behind me now
That'll dry in time
But there's always another fear, showing me how
I'm selfish and unkind
But it's your last touch that holds me now
While life escapes my mind
It's your last touch that holds me now
When life draws the line
There's one more tear inside me now
Always there to remind me how
Always there to remind me now

The Waiting Room

I only borrowed this body
At least, that's how I think of it
Now that I'm almost done with it
It treated me far better than I have it
Embracing me, instead of abandoning me
Like many, who knew better to leave
Though I'm surprised it didn't expire
Long ago, by its own desire
Instead it pulled me through and endured
Though it never found love, of that I'm sure
But I need to rest it now, by the window
As I ponder how things would have been
If I'd been kinder to it, gentler to it,
If I'd filtered some of the sin.
I should have seen it coming,
When my father's lung collapsed, I had a cigarette
I should have seen it coming,
When my brother succumbed to liver disease
I drank all night, perhaps all week
I still drink heavily
I should have seen it coming,
When a lover passed of HIV
I cried for him, I cried for me
Though some are still sexually active
Thinking luck's, a prophylactic.
I'm just borrowing this body, the one I rest in now
And when they come to fetch it, and they will
I hope they're not too offended, with how I've mistreated it
At least it never killed, even when it had the shot,
I wonder, will they see all the joy it brought me
A life lived in every line, in every blotch
In every scar and story,
Though some I've conveniently forgot
I know this body is not mine
And that it never truly was
But it did what I wanted it to,
But now it does what it does

And usually unexpectedly
Things I'd never think to do, at least not publicly
I try to sleep in the breeze
To the fading beat inside of me
Cause there's no here, here, now,
That was an earlier hour,
So, now I wait to see, which comes first
My last breath, or the doctor and the nurse
But this body was more than I deserved.
I think I hear them coming now
Approaching coupled feet
Growing closer and closer now,
Like a dying heartbeat.
This body that I've grown so used to
Never got used to me
Though it's less defiant now, as I grow weak
The prognosis in the fading light
Says I'll be trading it now,
Like day for night

The Other Side of The Door

Don't say something now, before you go
Why break your silence now?
Take your heart and nothing more
To the other side of the door
I remember back at the start
You were easier to please
Maybe time tore us apart
Perhaps it'll ease these memories
But now caught in the dark
I'm still choosing to breathe
And no matter what you believe
I still want you to leave

If It Would Help

Is there still time to save myself and show you someone else?
I'd show you someone else if it would help
I'd even lie if it would help
It's the way you look at me and make me see myself
I'd show you someone else if it would help
I could even try if it would help
There's enough that's tough in life and never felt
I'd show you someone else if it would help
I could even fly if it would help
I'd show you things you've never seen if it would help
I'd even show you someone else to save myself if it would help
I'd do all these things if it would help
I'd do all these things to save myself
If it would help

Should Have Seen It Coming

If we'd focused our fears
Then we wouldn't be here dying
But I never saw it coming

You abandoned the truth
Which took me further from you
Confused, I couldn't see it coming

You're like a dream
Where nothing's as it seems
Even thought, I saw you and me, it's funny
Though I should have seen it coming

But now, now it's too late
It'll never be the same
I should have seen it coming
Should have seen it coming

Out of My Mind

There was just too much,
Noise, you know
So, I had to go...
Out of the doorway,
Out of the city,
Out of your mind
It was just too rough
Inside, you know
You never reached, out for love,
Out to touch, out for us
There was just too much, 'Look at me!'
There was just too much, selfishness
There was just too much, let him bleed
There was just too much, loneliness
There was just too much, you need
There was just too much, B.S. between us
There was just too much, you never had enough
It was just too far, from the dream
There was just too much, you couldn't see
It was just too much,
For me

The Kiss

I doubt I even remember how to kiss
Though I do remember being good at it
At least from time to time
With the right lips, the right love
The right state of mind
And of course, the right words
Each determined by the other
Some filled with lies
Some set the world aside
Each so different, each determined
By the fate of night

No Matter What You Do

You limit your illusion when your lipstick lies to me
Cause it's not just your beauty that I need to hold closely
But when their words cause confusion
Why couldn't you side with me?

I know we don't find the same things amusing
And that it's not the way it used to be
But it only adds to the intrusion
Even if you don't mean to hurt me
I won't let this be our undoing
As cruel as it seems

Cause I'll still be there for you
No matter what you do

They say my face shows the bruises
And that I'm a sight to see
It's amazing what we go through
For a taste of ecstasy
I've never been one that loses
But nothing's guaranteed

But I'll still be there for you
No matter what you do

While Missing You

I need to walk,
Through the empty spaces
To be certain you're gone
Walking from room to room
As I feel the vacant draft cut thru
If not, I'd continue searching for you
Waiting for you, expecting you,
As I often do,
While missing you

On Getting Away

It's time to get away
Even familiarity
Doesn't seem familiar
These days
I could be anywhere
For all the comfort
And ease I feel here
I'd get away
If it weren't for the weather,
Or the money
Or other things, out of my control
So, I stay,
Even as the years
Stare back at me
With an odd and strange,
And not so soothing face,
Perhaps a face
That was once mine
Or perhaps because
I'm out of love,
With this city,
Though I'm sure
She's just as pretty,
As she ever was
But still, maybe
It's time to get away
To another place,
Before it
Offers yet another
Meaningless embrace,
Forcing me to dance
To some gay feng shui.
So, I turn to myself
But even these words,
Seem absurd,
So, I stay

Doorway in The Rain

Do you still see, the city I see?
Do you still have an address for me?
Or has it all changed, gone with the dream?
Do you still think about me?

Or have you moved on, to a new town?
Has love swept you away?
Or has life seen better days?
I loved your ways

Do you still look at life the same,
Caught in your doorway in the rain?
You loved the rain
You always loved the rain

Do you still laugh, the same laugh,
Like the one we shared in the bath?
Or has time taken that away?
I loved those days

Or has it all changed, gone down with a plane?
Has time taken you away?
Or were you washed away in the rain?
Funny, you always loved the rain

Do you still look at life the same,
Caught in your doorway in the rain?
You loved the rain
You always loved the rain

Familiar Rooms

(From the eponymous short story)

I never thought I'd see you again
Can't even remember how long it's been
Since you slammed the door that day
But when I saw you standing there
It was almost like before, in a way
You knew the room when you walked in
Sure, you knew the room
Christ, it slept me and you
Though now, it's a lot less cruel,
You said so many things
As you toured, and touched, and teased, the remains
In search of memories,
Perhaps even remembering a dream
You said, 'I see not much has changed,
Even your clothes are the same'
Then feigning surprise
You said, 'Well, perhaps not the same size'
You seemed so satisfied, even glorified
That there wasn't another woman in my life
So, with the room free of perfume
You'd thought to make your move
I watched you make your move
But remember, it's me
So, it's not too hard to see
You trying to dance a new design
Hoping you'd find
A familiar room
With a familiar fool
But what you failed to recognize
Was the presence of another guy,
One about the same size
You look like you could use,
A glass of wine

It'll Never Be So

Love is a place
You'll never go
No matter what you see
It'll never be so
No matter what you believe
You'll never know
No matter what you need
You'll just think so

Though
I hope it never mattered to you
It'd be too cruel
Cause I love in a place
Where you'll never go
A place with no doors
One you can't dress for
It's so much more
So much more
Then you'll ever know
Cause for you, it'll never be so
No, it'll never be so

I hope it never mattered to you
It'd be too cruel
Cause love's a place, you'll never go
You'll just imagine it
Poor soul
You'll just imagine it's so
That's all

Defenestrated Love

You never changed
You said you'd never change
So why was I surprised
That last night-
You cried, 'They're trying to-
Hold my life down!
Hold my life down!'

I never let you go
But a thousand nights closed
When you went out that window
With just your hair left in my hand
Taking everything,
I'll never understand

You screamed,
'I'm breaking myself now! Breaking myself now!'
As you hit the ground
Six floors down, into the ground
Six feet now

You let it all go
Why I don't know

Make me my own, (make me my own)
Make me feel strong, (make me feel strong)
Help me hold on, (help me hold on)
I'm going on now,
So long, for so long
So long

It's the Blues

It's the blues, I've been breathing
I gave up resisting
Did I wait a lifetime for this?
For this emptiness?
A faded kiss
Friends, I miss
You see, it's the blues I keep living
When people keep disappointing
Insisting they're self-important
In this lying culture
No promise of a future
With smiles that confuse you
Paying some dues
You end up losing, and you'll
Be just another user
And I keep telling you
It's the blues, I've been breathing
I gave up resisting
Did I wait a lifetime for this?
For this emptiness?
A faded kiss
Friends, I miss
It's the blues I keep greeting
It's my whole conversation
It's my close relation
Cause life is suffering
When people stop giving
And I just keep singing
Cause nothing's changing
Don't ask me what's new
It's the same old blues

I've waited a lifetime for this
For this emptiness

Rising Sons

I'm not my father's son
You see I've never hit a woman
Or argue by punching anyone
No, I'm not that person
I'm the man you couldn't see
The one you tried to take from me
The one you'll never meet
I'm the man you'll never be

And I'm sure you don't realize
Just how much you lost that night
Making my mother cry
Bruising her beautiful eyes
Good-bye

I'm not my mother's son
Making young girls come
You know, you can't go on
Pleasing everyone
Cause the little boy you see
Well, you see, he isn't me
He's back on some bloody street
Beaten by boys he couldn't be
Ma, don't cry

Today I have a son
His life threatened more than once
A life so filled with love
One some look down upon
But when it's said and done
They'd forgive my father's crime
And pray mine won't become
Won't become his father's son
Why?

Some Things Sometimes

I caught up with you, just the other day
Caught up to the dream
But I was so caught up in other things
There were things I forgot to say

I wanted to say, you seemed so unchanged
You even smiled the same
I could see, it's been good to you
I could see, that got you through
But I missed you

Now I wonder what it would have been like
If it'd been different that night
I wonder why I sacrifice
Some things, some things sometimes

Life's a close friend of mine
But sometimes, I don't know my own lines
Sometimes, we let go of ourselves,
And sometimes, someone else,
We just can't help
No, we just can't help

I caught up with myself, just the other day
I finally recognized the face
I was so caught up in other things
I'd lost my way
But I'm here today
It's clear today
In fact, it's sunny today

Before Too Long

You hit the road before dawn
You said, you had to move on
You always saw the world as wrong
And thought that love was too tough to hang on
But there were those nights, when you wouldn't let go
And those mornings, you held on for more
You can't always get, the dream every day
Or expect it not, to sometimes to slip away
You know who I am, you know where I'll stay
Waiting for you, and the love that we made
He hit the road, before dawn
He said, he had to move on
But like before, and like before
I hope he'll be back,
Before too long

Something's Wrong

Something's wrong,
It shows in your eyes
Save your disguise
There's nothing I won't understand
Always a friend, right to the end
But what are the words, to cover the pain?
To give hope again
Wish I could show you the way
But what can I say, we live day to day,
Just don't kiss it goodbye, it's a marvelous life
Though not always right
You can soar through the clouds
Rediscover yourself,
Or somebody else
Just remember the times,
That you loved how you felt

It's Just One of Those Things

I guess
I've been dreaming
All these years
That, or the dreams
Have just disappeared
I know some of my face,
Was lost on the way
And I'd recognize my soul,
If it ever looked the same
Sleeping with whores,
When it could've been better
He goes out the door,
In a borrowed leather
Crossing the street,
While counting his change
When death runs a red light,
Finally calling it a day
Good morning abuse,
I see, you're in bed again
Make-up in the mirror,
Trying to cover the pain
Crying, 'what's the use?'
Screaming, 'when does it end?'
Do you see yourself
In the eyes of a friend?
I guess we can drift,
Through all our fears
Unless we allow
Them to get too near
But then why do you say,
Through the bottom of a beer
'It's just one of things,'
When it's actually
Ten of your years?

Regret

You can't break a heart
That's broken its own
When most opportunities
Are lost and gone
But the very worst thing
To do that was wrong
Was never truly being
Your own person
You've lived a lot of life
And you've lived a lot of lies
Never really, a contender
Never really, in the fight
You only dreamed
Your hearts desires
When you put out the light
What cruelty you're caught in
Now that the truth is justified
While you're counting regrets
Regrets keep coming around
And you won't change anything
Moving from town to town
You're adding up regrets
And regrets are worse than sin
It's your own damned destination
Cause they're beginning again
The storm pounds the pavement
And the streets are flying by
It's the same old arrangement
You know it's always closing time
And no amount of cocktails
Or mother's fairy tales
Will make it any easier
When regrets have
Got you nailed

Running Home

Hey don't you know
When you're walking all alone
That baseball bats break bones
More than players running home

Chasing down the street
Confused adolescent machines
Welcome to the land
Free from persecution

They lied, they lied, they lied
Oh, how they lied!

When blood and concrete meet
Through biblical bigotry
One in prayer, one in fear
We all end on our knees

Blind, spineless, so mindlessly,
'God hates fags!' They scream

But how can God hate
When they say, God is love
Then hate must be manmade
And man, must give it up

Enough is enough is enough!
You're not the judge on judgement day!

They die, they die, they die,
Oh, why'd they die!

Waited A Life for This

We're brought up to live,
Such linear lives
Always coping with,
What's wrong and right
Dreaming some mischief,
In a restless night
Always wondering if,
It'll ever be paradise
Sometimes a lonely world,
Won't give what you deserve
It's not always boy and girl,
No matter what you've heard
But the crime is in the crying,
And not loving before dying
Or living a life of lying,
Just don't deny it
Cause you can see
What it all means
In the scheme of things
You're going to need
More than just dreams
More than dreams
In this mystery
I waited a life for this,
This meeting this myth
That I must confess,
I never thought to exist
I waited a life for this,
This one perfect kiss
But it's more than
Just your lips,
It's more
Religious

The Truth Is Strange to Me

We're lying in the gutter,
We're lying to each other
Don't tell me the truth,
The truth is strange to me
(Yes, it's strange to me)
There's the taste of something bitter,
On my bitten lip
I whisper unwillingly,
When your kisses are strange to me
(Deny your lies to me)
Determined and disgusted,
So cruel when we discussed it
I'm mean and wild, the killed child,
Confused with you chained to me
(There's a change in me)
I've lost the feeling in my fingers, (I've lost)
You've lost the light in your eye (the lights are out)
We've nailed each other senseless,
We're the crime that's crucified (we're all crucified)
An end without kindness (no kindness at all)
No reflection or shame (can't see myself)
And like before you'll cry out something
But it's still not my name (I've got no name)
Still lying in the gutter, (face down in the mud)
You're lying to another (it's never enough)
Don't tell me the truth, (no, not the truth)
The truth is strange to me (yes, it's strange)
Because of you (I'm crucified)
Because of you (I won't survive)
The truth is strange to me
You know the truth
'No, not the truth?'
Truth is strange to me
(I'm alone here)
Yes, it's strange to me
(I'm out of here)

Other Rooms

There's not a selfless person in the room
I gave up long ago on me and you
Be true a soul to see me through-
Funny in time I think less of you
As I recall your lies were cruel
Now sweeter tones in other rooms-
The other day I felt a whisper in my ear
The morning sun just drawing near
Unlike those distant sounds, it was sincere-
But I dreamt it was all just a dream
Can you see how tragic that would be?
I hope you dream without me-
Cause I know your room
Is still doubtful and dark,
Where even the shadows fall apart,
No place to leave a heart,
And no room to confuse, that it was all about you
To think, I used to dream about you

Within an Inch

She said, to tell you the truth
If you'd had just another inch or two
I'd have stayed with you, forever
I'd have overlooked anything else
And stayed with you. I hate myself for saying this
For needing it as I did
But I won't emasculate you, God forbid
I loved you, really, I did
But I needed that extra inch
And even saying it, is probably a sin
I know I'll regret it some day
But I'm not that person today
But I'll always think of you,
Within an inch or two

Can You Come Any Closer?

Can you come any closer?
Life doesn't feel the way it's supposed to
Down inside I'm alive
Fighting a frightening life

Can you understand my emotions?
I'm not the one who'll expose you
Just a soul, all alone
Trying to see Paris from the phone

One day before you die
You'll realize
You have to cry
To feel alive

Can you come any closer?
Whisper sweetly, gentle poetry
Press my lips, touch my chest
Put those fears to rest

Can you come any closer?
This doesn't feel the way it's supposed to,
You've rejected me
The little that's left of me

One day when you cry
You'll realize
There's no time
To live your life

Can you come, closer?

Goodbye

There's a look on your face
One I've seen nearly every place, I go,
From pulpit to picture show
In mirrors, I don't know
In smiles that won't grow

Now there's no reason to hang around
Eluding truths you haven't found, yet,
Caught in constant regret
Crying behind your cigarette
Won't get what you expect

I hate the tangled sheets beneath your tangled lies
I hate that you've wasted my precious time
And I hate that I still feel the need to feel you, inside

Though I hope I cross your mind
When it's all, well… behind you
Like life in the rearview
The blues a faded blue
The sunrise overdue

I hate the tangled sheets beneath your tangled lies
I hate that you've wasted my precious time
And I hate that I still feel the need to feel you, inside

But that's life
Goodbye

Would It Have Been So Bad?

Would it have been so bad, to just let it go?
Would it have been too much, to have left it alone?
Wasn't it truly tough?
Didn't you find the crying rough?
Didn't you think she'd had enough?
A blow to a bruise is truly cruel
And still she ran after you
Too in love to feel abused
Do you even know the hurt you do?

Would it have been so bad, to have eased the pain?
Would it have been too much, to have shown some shame?

Wasn't it really tough?
Didn't you find the crying rough?
Didn't you think she'd had enough?
But it's all just a joke to you
'What's red and white and black and blue?'
What you call love is really abuse
And no one comes to her rescue

Wasn't it really tough?
Didn't you find the crying rough?
Didn't you think she'd had enough?
And still, you're the dream come true
With a really poor attitude
And a selfish point of view
You think you're cool, but you're just confused

Would it have been so bad, to have tried to understand?
Would it have been so bad, to have just really cared?
To have just really cared?

Within the World Without the World

Within the world, without the world
Love is more than just a girl
It's something that truly works
Sometimes whispered and never heard

There's no mind in shooting stars
We must live with what we are
Watch the sky and realize
We can make our own lives

See some reason, show some light
Concentrate, and use your mind
Allow mysteries you can't hide
Don't fall karmic-ly behind

We stand back and watch great men
Most in ruin without friends
But somewhere deep within
You'll see Gandhi and Lennon

Within the world, without the world
Love is more than just a girl
It's something that shouldn't hurt
And more intrinsic than a word

Through Someone Else's Eyes

The beauty you desire, is designed by another's eyes
And when you call yourself, an individual,
You better cop to that compromise

You're adding up regrets
Through a thousand white lies
And finding your choices
Are a socially accepted disguise

It's hard to decide
You tried, till you cried yourself dry
And when you crawl, you see from where you fall
You better stop and realize

You'll end with regrets, and a thousand lonely nights
And finding your voice is
Doing more harm, than right

You ain't seeing, you ain't loving, you ain't feeling
When you're living, through someone else's eyes

And when you die
You won't turn into a butterfly
And that's all
You can't change what you did before
You better drop all those lies

And when you feel a death, nothing truly matters in life
It's just you and the forces
Everything else is blind

You ain't seeing, you ain't loving, you ain't feeling
When you're living, through someone else's eyes

After You

I feel your love
I feel your moods
It's all so close
And confused
Never thought, I'd go
After you
I wear your clothes
I drive your car
I live the life
You left behind
Trying to find
Something
To ease my mind
Even my tears
They come in twos
An empty bed
An empty room
It's all so hard
Living
After you
Your spirit's here
I feel nowhere
What once was real
Has disappeared
But life's something
To be shared
So, I'm going on
I'm going through
I'll pass the pain
Right to the dream
And after time
I'll be
I'll be, after you
After time
I'll be
Right after you

If This Is Love

If this is love
Then why's your touch
Feel so removed?
Or is love just something
That we do?
Who kisses who?
Who gives to whom?

If this is love
Why doesn't it feel like it should?
Like an old Hollywood film would
Where the kiss is good,
And love is understood

If this is love,
Why's it so tough?
Restless and rough,
What is this love?
Will it always be so confused,
Or turn out to be something true?
Should I find someone new,
And not be the fool?

Is this love?

Call It a Night

The nightclubs closed, awaiting the dawn
Am I going for someone or going alone?
No magic here, or mystery in the air
I know when it's right, and not lust at first sight
Before it gets light
Should probably call it a night

How many more bars, and morning scars,
That scare me and my visions away?
Where's that one that interests me,
With interests that I agree?
Before it gets light
Should probably call it a night

Some say reality is mostly unseen
Better make believe, believe with me
I need to change what I criticize
Last one to bed, I'm the first one to rise
Before it gets light
Should probably call it a night

You can't feign love, make big demands
Waiting for that special man
The right perfume, the perfect tan
Won't make you the perfect woman
Before it gets light
Should probably make it tonight

Inspiration

When it comes and I recognize it
For what it is
I run with it

Sometimes it's impossible to capture
And only sometimes embrace

I run with it
As an intended receiver going long

I run with it
Like a scooped by-line

I run with it
Like breaking news

I run with it
Sometimes, I even run towards you

Until the run-on sentences
Running on and on, stop running

I run with it
Until the glass is dry to the bone

I run with it
Until the inspiration is gone

Then I run with it
Until I'm done with it

Uncertainty

She'll cry
She'll give what's due
She'll make believe on you
Don't question things
That make no sense
She'll stare at you in silence

You dream she's sweet
But as with dreams
You'll wake to feel
You're incomplete
What uncertainty

Alone you'll wait
She'll hesitate
Un-promised love
No future stake

Those guessing games
Make life a shame
Uncertain things
Drive you insane

An ego bruised
A lesson learned
An edge to love
A victim burned

Uncertainty
Such
Uncertainty

It All Escapes Me

I wrote these lines of you this morning
Sitting in my broken room
A casualty, the day you left me
My name escapes me

Digging deeper into my wound
Someone passed with your perfume
I always dreamt with your perfume
Its name escapes me too

Closed all the windows, the sun went down
A mile of my mind crossed figuring out
How lucky I breath, no difficulty
It all escapes me, no doubt

I'll always remember that very first kiss
And your finger silencing the words on my lips
Sometimes when the light, and the night, are just like this
I know the memories I miss

When the Ending Came

Hey boy, on that dismal day
I knew we felt the same way
But I hated leaving you in the rain, anyway
When the ending came,
We nearly saw eye to eye
Enough to recognize
Enough to tell the time
Enough to keep it sane
When the ending came,
But the wild touches,
And even wilder kisses
Will always shine above the misses
Perhaps that even eased the pain
When the ending came

Finding You - Losing You

"You couldn't wait for me?"
"I thought you'd never come"
"So, what, you went with a woman?"
"Like I said, I thought you'd never come
What was I to do?
I waited years for you"
"But this? Why this?"
"It was the kiss, the wish
That caught me and took me in"
"But this? This?"
"She filled a place in me
We were both alone, and lonely
And nothing else, truly nothing else
Felt like home to me
I finally felt something inside
The emptiness was so…
You see, otherwise I would have died"
"And this is what you want?"
"Not what I wanted all along
But something I've committed to
Something I had to do
Something I couldn't find in you
Well, perhaps not you
But what was offered at the time
You don't understand
Love is so dubiously designed
And I couldn't get past the vanity I met
It was flighty and just physical, as you'd expect
It made love seem impossible
Uneventful, unsuccessful
But now you're here to prove me wrong
And say that I hadn't waited very long
Or long enough
But you don't know, it's been tough"
"You don't think I haven't gone through
The same as you?
The sky hasn't always been blue

I too have weathered a storm or two
But unlike you, I saw them through
And now here we are, and what are we to do?
At least tell me you've told her the truth?"
"That wasn't something I was going to do"
"You were going to lie, and cause more pain?
That isn't necessary, not again
Not anymore, certainly not like before
When religion was cause to blame
For women pained in false marriages
With their doctrines and cries of sin
But now getting back to that
To the other,
What are we to do?"
"I can't imagine losing you"
"I found finding the truth
Is as easy as telling it, but to tell you the truth
I don't know what to do, either"
"But I love you" "I love you too"
"I should have waited for you"

That Bridge

You're the only bridge I ever burnt
I can still see the smoke in the distance
A thick haze on the horizon,
Even after all these years
Still effecting the air, I breathe
And the things I need
The breath I lost because of you
And still do without you
But isn't that what we do?
What we've always done
Isn't that the view
We always become?

Fish in The Sea

Don't listen,
Don't believe
When they tell you,
There are always more fish in the sea
The truth is, there's fewer than you think

And even if you cast your lure efficiently
You'll find it filled with vanity and greed
And traces of clever deficiency
That only help to deceive,
There are no more fish in the sea

I've crossed an ocean in search of it
I've crossed a country for it
I've crossed a road,
Thinking I recognized it
I even thought I'd caught wind of it
But there are no more fish in the sea

I've crossed a smoky room too
Not certain what I'd do if it were you
Having been doubled-crossed a time or two
I even questioned the menu
There are no more fish in the sea

Not genuinely.
So, I'm forced to concede
It'll never get
Its hooks in me

A Chilly Winter's Moment

Reflecting on a vague and dying light,
A chill that still holds me tight
Nothing grows, not even the dwarfed image of me,
Not the moss on trees, or even trees
Dying trunks in a dying breeze, as they age
On an empty winter page, a palm of poetry
Tossed like madness into the sea, with rage
Without a moment of hope and desire
I fail to find warmth, even by the fire
My close breath, feels more like death
As it freezes on the chilly windowpane
Don't kid me in this emptiness,
Not again, even a summer's dream, I miss
Just thinking about it, living without it
Left behind, murdered by nature, torn by time
In the bare and brittle clearing, I see
Long shadows, fingers reaching for me
I can't fail to recognize,
A hopeless future filled with lies,
It's too dark, even for winter,
In this heated hell, I'm cold and bitter
This is what you bring
As I wait and pray for Spring

The Art in Dying

I woke this morning, without you
At a loss at what to do, without you
A sad day, as sad day's go, it's sadder even still
As the air around me, barely gets me through
A quiet morning, even a year past now
The music continues, as do you
In a moment of crying, to one of your tunes
I can feel your art in dying,
As it fills the room

The City by The Bay

I ran into an old memory again,
More an old friend
That reminded me of you,
In a café, close to Vesuvio's,
You know, one of those,
One you can't plug into,
Like before the internet
When things were more intimate,
An actual place, where you met,
The love of your life,
If just for the night
And you didn't even have to swipe right
It had an interesting face, an interested face
One a soul could embrace
If not relate to, or fall in love with
Back when streets were less congested
And the skyline hadn't yet been molested,
Now that was a view,
Most photos couldn't do, justice
When we lived, as if in, a foreign film,
Matinees, for days, filled, with romance
When you helped an old lady with her cart
And you could actually park
And cars stopped in crosswalks
And newspaper columns were works of art
When taxi drivers were writers,
(and not always on their cell)
With colorful tales to tell
When film festivals were accessible
And you could touch a star atop a hill
In old San Francisco.
I miss you, old girl,
Keep well

Your Hand

Where is your hand
When it's not in view?
Where is it,
And what does it do?
The one, once tucked
Between me and you
Has it done
Something scandalous?
To bring it to ruin,
Something
It shouldn't have been doing
Has it taken something
It shouldn't?
Another heart perhaps,
Or a broken room?
Or another,
It couldn't commit to?
I can only imagine,
Where it's been now
And what it's been shaking
Or even the love
It's been making,
But I wish it would have
Told me
Or given me a sign
That it could no longer
Hold me,
It would have been
The fair thing to do

Mattress-cide

I lay on the mound at the center of the bed
Expecting to roll one way or the other as I slept
Wondering whose side, I'd be sleeping on, or curling into
Who slept on the right, and who on the left?
And what did they do, or didn't do, in this motel room?
Its history, I'm caught between
Were there moans? Were there dreams?
I tested each dip as I did,
Seeing how well I'd fit into it, as one seemed bigger than
The other. And where was the sex, where was the shared ground
Certainly, not on the plateau I was balanced on
Did one make a move, while the other quietly waited
Waiting for the other to cross the line
I lay upon, on that great divide
Like a barrier, keeping each to their side. Or were these
Just pits of solitude, without even a honeymoon. Cause the valleys
Ran so deep, and the wall stood so tall
I expected to fall, one way
Into someone's lonely world, or perhaps into the other
A sleepless night, one filled with want, with need,
With desire, and lost memories
Still resting there, still buried there
Even now on these freshly laundered sheets
These thoughts kept my own sleep suspended on that heap,
But I'd have taken a different path,
One not without a laugh
Or I'd never go back again, I wouldn't dare
I'd have just left you there,
Coffee to go, with keys on the bureau
I'd have parked the car under the vacancy sign
Without a word, but satisfied
Both free to go, without leaving a note,
Since everything that needed to be said, had been said
And didn't need to be said again.
These tortured images brought a restless
Sleep to my head
(My own past, dying somewhere in a distant bed)

And when I woke, in that motel room,
My body feeling like hell in a tomb
It would seem I'd fallen asleep,
Balanced well above those challenged sheets
As if on a pitcher's mound
Waiting to throw the first ball out,
Fast, hard, or slow
The errors are always so difficult

Being Proud

I'm walking away
But I want to turn around
But I know what you'll say
So, I'm forced to be proud
It's enough to know
We could let love go
But not enough
To keep the love that we know
I'm walking away
Still I want to turn around

A Matter of Time

We're caught here in time
Somewhere between good and goodbye
A fading smile, an occasional lie
It's just a matter of time
My guess is, the best is, behind us
Now with three or four of us, in the mix
Somewhere between good and goodbye
It was just a matter of time
Before that love,
Became a crime

This Time

As he lit his cigarette,
He stared him straight in the eye,
He couldn't deny, he was attractive,
And probably foolishly shy,
But he was cautiously tempted
As he drew the smoke into his lungs
Thinking, if things were different,
What might they have done
Since he was just as young, and innocent
Perhaps it was even a face he'd once met,
Somewhere more discreet, no less
But in his eyes, he saw many faces,
Just as close as his, if not closer,
Lighting his cigarette, nearly the same
Some flirtatious, some sincere
Some just passing through, their intentions clear
He smoked his first with an older sister
On the stoop of their flat, in Upper Manhattan
A few days later they shared another,
Just as their mother, walked by,
And as was common in the Sixties,
Though still a dubious decision
She gave his twelve-year old sister permission
To join her in the living room, for a smoke or two
As they watched the old black and white tube
A week or so later, his sister said
In a parental tone, and from then on,
That he was much too young
Though, she'd been the one who'd turned him on,
So, at the cruel age of eight, he quit and went straight
Until he started up again, in his late teens
It was just one of those things,
You did, like drinking in bars,
Where he was often considered a star
Where night after night, someone lit, his cigarette,
Hoping to steal his young breath,

And there were those endless nights after sex
Smoking the obligatory cigarette
Then recently, at a party, unlike any before,
For at this one, the authorities kicked down the door
No one's ever pleased to see the police
Especially in the Middle East,
It just proved how foolish he'd been,
Cause there was surely no worse place to meet men,
But now younger thoughts comforted him,
Though not as fresh as they'd once had been,
And as the desert sun was rising,
As in a cinematic dream
His cigarette ashes blew like dust in the wind
And when it finally came to the filtered end
He let the butt drop from his mouth,
And even thought to stamp it out
But then the expected shot rang out
And one last thought, crossed his mind,
'I'll surely quite this time'

Closer to You

You're still here with the morning sun
Still here, after I was wrong
Laying here, still, still with me
Closer than a friend to me
Closer than a memory
Holding you close,
Closer to me

Escape with Romeo

That wasn't love that held you
Or love that let you go
Love doesn't make you blue, like that
You should have escaped with Romeo

Walls on Both Sides

I live adjacent to a historic arthouse
Sharing a wall with it in fact
The vibrations, the cinematic scores
Even the bad reviews of course,
All carried through the cracks
They're playing a Stones' film now
It's like being backstage again
Sharing a rider as I did
All those nights at Winterland,
With The Dead
That's how it used to be
Back in the Seventies
But the sound is just as close
So close, that I expect the band
To bounce in after the show
But I've never seen the Stones though.
The music shakes the walls
It's a nice sensation,
Better than hearing the neighbors
And their amorous creation,
That sounds like love,
But it's not what it seems
Not surprisingly,
It's more a commercial scream
Cause sex for sex's sake,
Only impersonates,
That lover she dreams,
It's quiet now,
Now that it's over
Nothing to say to one another
Or if they do, it reignites a feud
The same from a week or two
The same as a year ago, as it always goes
It's the same though, when she mentions
Another man in comparison
Of course, it awakens his insanity,
I know it would me,

Thankfully, eventually,
They turn on the TV
But there's nothing really to see,
As you'd expect
Though it's a nice effect
When we watch the same show
It's like stereo.
Just then,
The concert roars up again
Old songs,
Rocking and rolling my bedroom walls
I can even smell the popcorn
Especially the butter
Everything's better with butter
Brando used it cleverly
I try and use it sparingly
I try and get some sleep
As the boys play
To my faded dreams

With You

It's better,
When the sun goes down
We have more in common, more of a connection
Something about the night, brings us closer to perfection
It's sweeter, it's better, it even tastes like Heaven
But in the light, that harsh light, you're a total stranger
Even your skin feels different, like danger
And the words, well, the words
They're not as delicious in the light,
They taste different in the light
More insipid, in fact,
But that's what I've come to expect
It's easier to see your lies in it
Something else, too, I thought it was me,
But it's you

A Younger Member, A Memory

At this age, I'm too romantic for hasty advances
He waits impatiently to show-off his talent,
And I'm glad to see that talent never changes,
Though maybe it's my own imbalance that makes it feel so dangerous
But then, it was a different life back then
But now I'm forced to play a part, I've never been
You see, I'd rather have shared his world with him
I wanted to, the way I once wanted you,
Wanting me, wanting him, still wanting you,
But I'm content in the measure, he offers to share,
It reminds me of mine, though mine took twice as long to get there
And when I finally swung my sword in his direction
It seemed nearly defenseless, more pensive,
More like a quill dipped in ink than fencing
But it meant more to me, than it used to, at least
And as he goes at it, with voluntary abandon, as young men do
He promises to be gentle, but I don't expect him to
It's inherent in his design, his very existence,
(Like it once was mine, we share that experience)
But as his unbridled blood reached its boiling point
It was more a memory than I thought, and when his seed is done,
Saving the world from extinction,
His last strokes are certainly worth honorable mention,
And I must admit, his enthusiasm was impressive,
Like a tempest tearing through history
Though I recall while clothed, he seemed less cocky
Uncertain, for sure, even reserved,
So, to say clothes make the man, is totally absurd,
Cause in his nakedness, he was a force to be reckoned with
Sadly, it ended all too quickly, that it seemed like a trick to me
(That wasn't meant to be funny)
But I'm forced to face, myself again, but now as a younger man
For the kudos and the crimes, and the passion in his reside,
Is exactly where I'd have been
But now I judge and criticize, being what I once defied
And even now deny, for I still see myself, in his young eyes

Be Yourself

They tell you to be yourself
'Just be yourself'
But when they don't like what they see
They tell you to be someone else
'Be someone else'
They tell me to be true to myself
'Be true to be yourself'
But in truth
They want me to be someone else
No wonder why, some kill themselves
They say, 'Be a man,
Be what you can'
But when they can't take what I am
They take what I am,
Why are you killing me, man?
They say, 'You've got to be free'
Then they tell me where to stand
I know where I stand
They tell me to live my life
But not as who I am
But more like them
Cause it's less threatening,
To be like them

Letting You Go

Forgive me for letting you go
But there was so much you didn't know
So much I was going through
So much I couldn't tell you
At the time
It's just better though, to let you go
Anything else,
Would have been a crime

I Don't Know What That Means

When you say, you love me,
I don't know what that means
Not from what I've felt, certainly not from what I've seen
It doesn't seem like that to me
When you say, you'll stick by me
I don't know what that means
Cause every time I turn around, you abandon me
When you say, you believe in me
I don't know what that means
Since when did you believe in anything
Do you even see what I see?
When you say, you know me
I don't know what that means
And when you say you're just like me
You scare me
Cause that's not me

Parted Lips

I can taste
The laughter on your lips
The little trace
The little that you left
I still taste,
I can taste
The love on your lips
The little trace
The little that you left
I still taste,
I can trace
The love on your lips
The little that you left
That sweet taste
That still goes well,
With a chilled chardonnay

I Like Skin

I like skin
From where it begins,
(Where it's genuine)
To where it ends
It's something you look sexy in
I like skin
I love the smell of it,
I love what you're wrapped in
Give me some skin
No matter what it's covering
I like skin
If it's covering me
Or covering him,
Into him
Into me, in me
Though sometimes
I wonder where it's been
Or I know where it's been
I like it warm, close under covers
I like it wet, straight from the shower
I like it when it sweats for hours
I like it when it smells like flowers
I like skin
It's nice to dream in
It's nice to be in
It's nice to lay next to
It feels nice on you
I like skin
Dwelling in it, searching in it,
Discovering it, feeling it
Crawling in it, or on it
Or crawling out of mine, to get to yours
It's the closest thing to living you
Feeling you, being you
I like skin
Pressing, caressing
Leaning into me, being me

Pressing, caressing
Leaning into you, being you
I like skin
I love the fragrance of it
Leading me, teasing me, everything
I like skin
It covers me, it covers him
And it even covered her once, back when
It lies with me, it lies within
I can still hear my young voice grin
'Give me some skin'
You see, I don't care where it's been
So, long as it sticks with me
Sticks to me
Like humidity
Skin me alive, I won't mind
When it comes between us, it comes alive
When it gets close enough, it is us
(I also like sin, on occasion)

Love Left Me Here

Like it leaves me everywhere,
Almost every time, no in fact, every time,
It's left me on a corner, contemplating my crime
Or reflected in a mirror crying
Love's always been denied
Scared, confused, confined
Another door closed, another left behind
Love left me here
Colder, and older now
Not even a shadow over my shoulder now
To search me out
Or a dry eye in the house
Love left me here
Just like it left me there,
Without you

Awoken

Something has happened to wake me from sleep
Perhaps something far away and out of reach
As the room lay quiet around me
Resting far better than me.
Perhaps something closer to heart
An intimate overdue for a visit on my part
I need to get out more, or at least start
It's just a feeling, as feelings will do
Pushing their way through
Though perhaps it's just something that I ate
That's unsettled and tastes like fate
There's something there though
That comes and goes from time to time
That unleashes me from sleep
Best to just turn over and let it be
Until the phone finally rings
Or someone texts me
At least that would settle the matter
And I could sleep

Laughing Gear

"She might as well have put her mouth around a joke as she spoke,
Shaking her head, she said, while turning away in bed,
'Don't expect me to put my laughing gear around that thing again.
You're out of your head.'
It wasn't her being overly impressed, as she might have once said,
But ignoring a sexual request, as women will do, after they've wed
And had a kid or two,
Leaving me to satisfy myself on the other side of the bed."
At least that's what he said, as his laughing gear quietly went dead.

My Audience Is Dead

Or quickly dying
I didn't kill them,
I only wish I could have
Been that effective, earlier on
But I let them sit too long
(Or perhaps, I sat too long)
Wilting away, expiring naturally
With time, or rather the changes of time
Or just plain changes
There might still be a few, a dying few
With fading eyesight
Or worse, fading mind,
The view, a lost view
Love undiscovered, or as elusive under covers
But sadly, that audience is dead now too
Though most died early on
If you recall the crime

Listening

It's interesting, listening
To others having sex, picturing
Their every move
Doing things, you probably wouldn't do
(Though I picture them with you)
I imagine her on top, since he's too lazy,
Besides, she has that attitude,
At times, too demanding, sometimes even rude
They're strangely more attractive now
Out of sight, with just the sound
They can't be finished, not so soon?
But there it is,
A quiet room

Earthquakes

We don't hang anything
Over our beds here
Not even crosses
Cause we know even crosses kill
Like anything else will
If you believe in them or not
Everything eventually falls in the dark
I was even double-crossed once
Nearly died
What was worse
It was an inside job
When they forced theology
Into me
Blindly
Interrogating me
Innocent me
Innocent you, too
If they got to you,
They still refuse to see
Those young bodies bleed
Mindlessly
Forced into me like a fathering seed
They fear free spirits in the world
Afraid
Boys will cross their legs like girls
You see, crosses kill
As they beat you at will
A sad truth
A blow to a bruise
Religious abuse
But then,
What's new?

Fume Funerale

It was sexy in the Sixties to smoke,
As sexy as a memory can be
Like sin in cinema,
Still living in our dreams
But now, it's just hard to breathe
And even this cadence is forced to concede
In limited velocity, to a shallow iambic left in me
It'll be the death of me, this lack of breath in me
Is all that's left of me,
Like a suicidal lover, under cover
Who'll easily kill you for another
Addicted to nicotine, I lit my first before my teens
Dreaming through clever smoke rings
And reflecting images on the silver screen,
Where a cool lean character leaned in faded blue jeans
A cigarette pack tucked under a sleeve
Of a freshly laundered tee,
Where he also hid his insecurities

That Could Have Been

Me, or rather, my younger self
As I saw him walking with someone else
At least it didn't look like you
In the dark shadows that afternoon
Obviously, he'd made better decisions
Something I wish I had done
As I watched him walk without derision,
To a life, I should have won
Rather, the one I dreamt of earlier on,
And if given the effort needed
That could have been me, indeed
And that world
Would have been mine
Given the time

Love Is but a Whisper

Between a room and rumor
Between love and a lie
Loving one moment, lying the next
Nothing is what you hoped for
Certainly, not what you'd expect
Cause what's near and dear to me,
Sears through me
And when love ignores me
(Literally and figuratively)
I'm forced to recognize
The agony inside
The lost fantasy, the altered destiny
Certainly, not the one I used to see
And when it ends, I've lost a friend,
All this,
From a whisper

I Remember It Well

It was the last day I was young and daring
The last time I would have done anything
No matter how stupid, how foolish
How ridiculous, like when we were kids
It often comes as a crime, or a resignation
For some it's a simple wrinkle,
An ache, or blind mistake
Sometimes it comes at half century
When you finally feel it in the knee
And need a change of pace
You learn to approach life cautiously
Expecting something to give out, or break
What was once second nature, is more a stranger now
And stranger still, it doesn't feel,
Like it'll get any better,
But you pray it will

You Meant That Much to Me

I was trying to make you feel special
I was trying for the truth,
I even denied myself a moment
Cause I'd have done anything for you
But you said, 'I'm not committed to anything these days'
But is that what you meant to say?
Sometimes we seemed so close,
And then there were those
Times, it was like fantasy,
You meant that much to me
But now it's just too hard to hang on
I lose my grip when the passion's gone
Just look what we've both become
Too many lies on too many tongues
And little more than words in a song
I tried to make you feel,
I cried for the truth,
I denied us nothing
Cause I'd have done anything for you

Don't Say Goodbye

Danced around a trick or two,
Lived a life of broken rules
But when you pulled away your arm
I knew something was wrong,
I knew you were through
In virgin attire or whorish disguise
I won't deny I was satisfied
I won't deny my dubious design
Don't part your lips to say goodbye
But to relive that kiss that night
The one that set the world aside
Don't say goodbye

I Missed You

I missed you, at your hotel
And as I write this song
I hope you travel well
Again, and against; time and romance
Another moment
And I'd have had the chance
To kiss you, just for awhile
And do certain things...
To make your heart smile
I missed you at your hotel
And as I sing this song
I hope you
Travel well

Surprisingly Strong

You say I'm strange,
Don't we all call each other that?
You say I've changed,
I'm glad that you noticed that
But you make me feel the same way
Cause I need no other way.
Love's surprisingly strong
Forever is for so long,
So long as we want forever
You're so surprisingly strong.
When I go wrong,
Don't you come right after me
You thought I was strong,
But don't you go and follow me.
Sometimes, we want more,
But we're not, we're not truly sure
It was so lonely before,
When my heart
Was nearly destroyed

Fade You Away

I pull on my passion,
Trying to fade you away
But all I can feel,
Is you're something so real
And I often wonder,
What kind of man I've become
Is there something you see,
That won't bring you to me?
Am I left in the dark now,
Feeling life's unbegun?
Can I turn it around,
Hoping I'll hear your sound?
I pull on my passion,
Trying to fade you away
But all I can feel,
Is you're something so real
Trying to fade you away,
Fade you away,
Fade you away

How Do You Feel?

How do you feel?
It's Sunday afternoon
Just me and you, in an empty room
We said so much, we told some lies
Pressed and promised, we felt something inside
How do you feel, now that the papers read?
How do you feel, now that the sun's gone down?
Did you find what I found?
How do you feel, now that we're all alone?
Now that the wine is gone
How do you feel?

Ciao

It was ciao in the beginning
And ciao at the end
One word for one moment
One moment spent
I'll remember you
And your love too
But now I'm ready to go-
Ciao!

www.ingramcontent.com/pod-product-compliance
Lightning Source LLC
Chambersburg PA
CBHW051847040426
42447CB00006B/730